21ST Century Skills Library

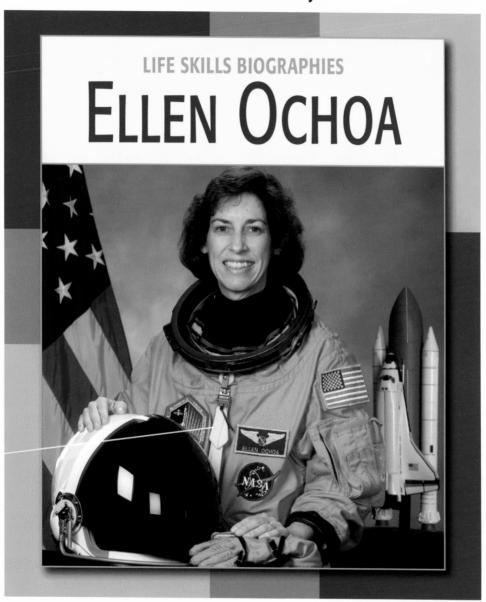

LIFE SKILLS BIOGRAPHIES

ELLEN OCHOA

Annie Buckley

Cherry Lake Publishing
Ann Arbor, Michigan

CHERRY
LAKE
Publishing

Published in the United States of America by Cherry Lake Publishing
Ann Arbor, MI
www.cherrylakepublishing.com

Content Adviser: Angela Posada-Swafford, Science Writer/Producer

Library of Congress Cataloging-in-Publication Data
  Ellen Ochoa / by Annie Buckley.
    p. cm.—(Life skills biographies)
  ISBN-13: 978-1-60279-075-9 (hardcover)
  ISBN-10: 1-60279-075-2 (hardcover)
  1. Ochoa, Ellen—Juvenile literature. 2. Women astronauts—United States—Biography—Juvenile literature. 3. Astronauts—United States—Biography—Juvenile literature. 4. Hispanic American women—Biography—Juvenile literature. I. Title. II. Series.
  TL789.85.O25B83 2007
  629.450092—dc22
  [B]   2007004467

*Cherry Lake Publishing would like to acknowledge the work of
The Partnership for 21st Century Skills.
Please visit www.21stcenturyskills.org for more information.*

Contents

INTRODUCTION

Have you ever wondered what it takes to become an astronaut? Ellen Ochoa did. When she was 11 years old, Neil Armstrong became the first man to walk on the moon. Fourteen years later, while Ochoa was studying at Stanford University, Sally Ride became the first American woman to travel in space. Finally, in January 1990, Ochoa had her chance. She was accepted into the National Aeronautics and Space Administration (NASA) training program, and in 1993, she became the first Latina woman to travel into space.

But she didn't become an astronaut overnight. Her journey is filled with hard work, perseverance, dedication, and the courage to follow her dreams—all the way into outer space.

Ochoa rose to the top of a very difficult career and is also a wife and the mother of two children. How did she overcome challenges and maintain her focus? How does she balance work and family, studies and fun? Two of the most important qualities she brings to everything she does are persistence and joy. She has always tried her best in school and pursued what she loves to do.

～

CHAPTER ONE

AN EXCELLENT STUDENT

Ellen Ochoa was inspired when she watched Neil Armstrong walk on the moon in July 1969.

Ellen Ochoa was born on May 10, 1958. Her parents, Rosanne and Joseph Ochoa, had five children, three boys and two girls. Ellen was the middle child. She grew up in La Mesa, California. Education was important to both of her parents.

When Ellen was still a baby, her mother started college. For the next 22 years, Rosanne took one class at a time until she completed her degree and graduated from San Diego State University. Growing up, Ellen

Many people wonder what it would be like to view Earth from outer space.

Life & Career Skills

Rosanne Ochoa took 22 years to graduate from college, but she did it—and with near-perfect grades! She had a 3.9 GPA (grade point average) and in 1982 graduated summa cum laude, which means with special honors, because of her grades. While in school, she told her children about what she was studying. Her enthusiasm for learning, good study habits, and hard work all had a big influence on Ellen and her siblings. Each of the Ochoa children graduated from college.

But Ellen's mother put her family first. She raised her five children while she was in school. When she graduated, her own mother became ill, and Rosanne took care of her. In 1985, Rosanne joined the staff of the Union-Tribune Publishing Company. She worked at the paper for 16 years in many different positions. Rosanne was very nurturing and loving, and she believed in higher education and better career opportunities for women. Ellen found an inspirational role model in her mother.

saw her mother reading, studying, and selecting diverse courses such as business, biology, journalism, and language. Her mother's decision to get a college degree (she eventually earned three degrees) and her commitment to her studies while raising five children were inspirational to Ellen and her siblings.

Ellen's father, Joseph, was in the navy and later was the manager of a retail store. He came from a Mexican American family. His parents moved to Arizona, where Joseph was born, from the Mexican state of Sonora. Joseph was the youngest of 12 children. He was raised in a bilingual household; they spoke both English and Spanish.

When Joseph was growing up, he and his brothers and sisters experienced discrimination. Because they were Latinos—which means they came from a Latin American culture—and spoke Spanish, some children made fun of them. This was difficult for Joseph, and when he grew up, he decided that he

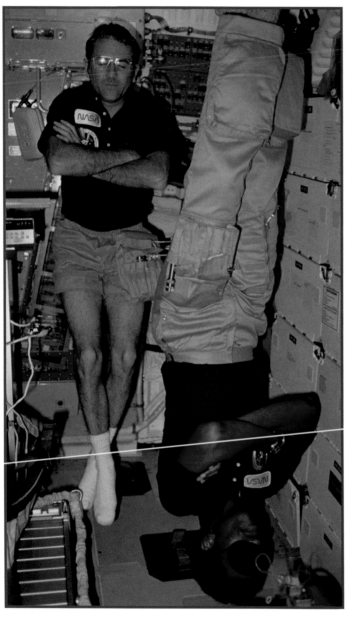

Guy Bluford (right) was the first African American astronaut. Like Ellen Ochoa's father and other Latinos, many African Americans have experienced discrimination.

would not teach his children Spanish. He wanted to do everything he could to protect them from the kind of discrimination he had experienced as a child. When Ellen was a little girl, she did not learn Spanish.

As a child, Ellen enjoyed reading and math. When she was 10 years old, she also learned to play the flute. From a young age, she was an excellent student. In both the seventh and eighth grades, she was voted most outstanding student in her school. At age 13, she won the San Diego County

Ellen Ochoa enjoys listening to and playing music.

Spelling Bee. As it turned out, these were only the first of many awards that Ellen would receive in her life.

When Ellen was in junior high school, her parents divorced. She and her siblings lived with their mother after the divorce. While such a big change can cause some children to lose their focus, Ellen maintained her concentration in school and on her music. She was developing into a great flute player.

Ellen continued her scholarly success and soon began high school. At Grossmont High School, she studied calculus, an advanced math class, and was voted the school's top musician. She could have taken chemistry and physics, but decided against it. At that time, she was not interested in science.

Ellen's mother also taught her children to follow their dreams and study whatever interested them. So Ellen took many different courses and continued to play the flute. In 1975, because she had the highest grades in her graduating class, she was the class valedictorian. This meant she would give a speech at graduation.

After high school, Ellen was offered a scholarship to attend Stanford University, one of the top-ranked colleges in the United States. But she decided not to take it and instead stayed near home to attend San Diego State University. She wanted to be near her family so she could help her mother.

Ellen began college with a major in music, but she switched her major five times. She chose business, journalism, and computer science before choosing a science major. She wanted to explore ideas and find something she loved before settling on one subject. Finding what she really enjoyed was important. Ellen believes that enthusiasm and motivation are just as important as hard work. She says, "You need to be interested in what you're doing and willing to work hard, even if you encounter obstacles."

CHAPTER TWO

FINDING FOCUS

Ellen Ochoa attended San Diego State University.

In college, Ochoa continued to explore her many interests. One of the courses of study that interested her was electrical **engineering**, a field that applies the principles of electricity in a practical way to create things and invent new ways of building or designing. But at that time, few women worked in that field, and she was discouraged from studying to be an engineer. Instead she chose to major in physics—the science of matter and energy and the way they relate to one another. With her strong grades in math, she was admitted to the physics department, and in 1980, she earned a bachelor's degree.

Because she was at the top of her class, Ochoa was valedictorian at her graduation from San Diego State University, just as she had

Marie Curie won the Nobel Prize in Physics in 1903, when few women worked in that scientific field.

Stanford University opened its doors to students in 1891. Ellen Ochoa completed her master's degree there in 1981.

been in high school. Her family was very proud of her. She was pleased with her accomplishments but still unsure whether she wanted to pursue a career in music or in science.

Her mother encouraged her to continue her studies before deciding on a career, so Ochoa decided to apply to graduate school. Her hard work and high grades during her undergraduate years paid off. She received another scholarship offer from Stanford University, and this time she took it. The scholarship, called the Stanford University Engineering Fellowship, validated her earlier interests because now she would have the chance to study engineering.

In the field of engineering, everything studied in the laboratory relates somehow to day-to-day life. Engineers apply what they learn in the laboratory to problems or situations outside of it. They need to be good at math and science, but they also need to be inquisitive and able to think critically and creatively about a problem in order to solve it. Ochoa, who had succeeded in many different subjects, was attracted to the diversity of skills needed for engineering.

Stanford University is in northern California, and to attend, Ochoa moved farther from home than she had ever lived. When she got to Stanford, she discovered that she was one of the few women in her classes. Though she enjoyed her studies, it was lonely being one of the only women in the department.

Her positive outlook and flexibility helped her through this difficulty. She tried out for a position with the Stanford Symphony Orchestra as a flutist,

Learning & Innovation Skills

While in college in San Diego, Ochoa was intrigued by a textbook written by a professor from Stanford named Ronald Bracewell. Bracewell was a physicist and electrical engineer, and Ochoa became interested in engineering. Eventually, she would go on to study and work with him.

Have you ever read a book or seen a picture or participated in an activity that was especially interesting to you? Paying attention to what interested her helped Ochoa find a job she loves—and a very exciting one, too!

and was accepted. Playing in the orchestra, she met new people and interacted with another community on campus. She stayed with the orchestra throughout her studies. In 1981, she won the Student Soloist Award, which is given to a student musician for outstanding performance on his or her instrument.

During her years at Stanford, Ochoa began to feel more comfortable in science classes, too—thanks in part to her finding a mentor, someone interested in her studies who could help her. Joseph Goodman was a Stanford professor and one of the leading experts in optics, or the study of light and how we see. The field had piqued her interest during her undergraduate studies.

With Goodman as her mentor and adviser, someone who helps students select classes and plan a course of study, Ochoa became excited about her graduate studies. In 1981, she earned her master's degree in electrical engineering and received another scholarship to continue studying electrical engineering.

That same year, NASA launched the first space shuttle, a reusable spacecraft that can launch into space and return to Earth. The *Columbia* orbited, or circled, Earth 36 times before safely landing. This was a huge achievement for the U.S. space program. Now astronauts could conduct scientific experiments in space, and scientists on Earth could study the results after the crew returned.

Meanwhile, Ochoa pursued a doctorate degree. This is the most advanced degree a scholar can earn in a specific field. In her doctoral research, she specialized in the field that continued to fascinate her—optics.

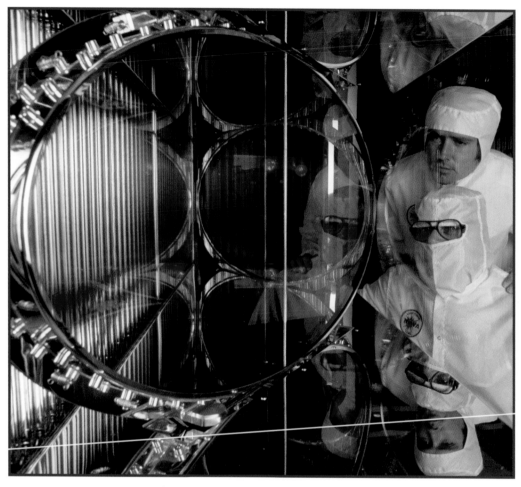

A technician inspects one of the lenses of a laser.

She conducted experiments to research and design optical systems using computers and other technology. Optical systems are an advanced way of using lasers or computer technology to "see." For example, some of the research she did led to new discoveries in laser eye surgery. Most of the projects she worked on studied ways that machines and robots could

detect objects, or "see." Many of these would help scientists conduct experiments in space.

Ochoa worked with Goodman and another professor, Bert Hesselink, to develop an entirely new optical inspection system. This system could find errors in a pattern. For example, a factory could use an optical system like this one to find problems or flaws in manufactured objects. The system might "see" that there is an error in a product just as people might use their eyes to detect this flaw. The team applied for a U.S. patent for the system. A patent is an official document granted by the government. It states that an invention is new and that the patent holders have the rights to the invention.

Ochoa was a coinventor on this patent and, since that time, has received patents for two other important inventions in the field of optics. One of them is for an optical system, or machine, that can recognize objects. The other is for an optical system that can take clearer pictures of objects once they are identified by the machine. Each of her patents is for an optical information processing system. This is a technical system that uses lasers or other materials to gather information from an object.

While Ochoa was conducting research, performing with the symphony, and playing volleyball for fun, there was another exciting development in the world of space travel. On June 18, 1983, Sally Ride became the first American woman to travel in space. She was a mission specialist on a space shuttle called *Challenger* that was in space for six days. The crew conducted research and positioned communications satellites in space for Canada and Indonesia. A satellite is a spacecraft that can orbit Earth

Challenger *was first launched into space on April 4, 1983.*

21st Century Content

It is very difficult to become an astronaut, but NASA accepts applications from qualified individuals regardless of their gender or cultural background. To apply to be an astronaut, NASA has some requirements. But even those who meet or exceed these requirements are not always accepted. There simply are not as many space flights as there are qualified applicants.

NASA requires applicants to have a bachelor's, or four-year college degree, in engineering, biological science, physical science, or mathematics. They must pass strict physical and psychological examinations. And they must have experience or a higher degree in their area of expertise, such as engineering or mathematics.

There are additional requirements for each position. For example, to be a pilot astronaut, applicants must be pilots with more than 1,000 hours of experience. To be a mission specialist astronaut, applicants must have at least three years of related professional experience or higher education, such as the master's and doctorate degrees in engineering that Ochoa received.

and collect information or do research. *Challenger* used a robotic arm, a type of robot that works just like a human arm does to reach or grab, for the first time.

Ochoa and her friends and classmates were excited about the space shuttle program at NASA. Seeing Sally Ride become an astronaut was inspiring. In 1985, Ochoa and some classmates decided to apply to the NASA Astronaut Training Program. She was turned down, but that same year, she received her doctorate in electrical engineering from Stanford University. This was a big accomplishment, and she was ready to go into the world and begin her career as a research engineer.

CHAPTER THREE

BLAST OFF!

*Space shuttles are launched from the Kennedy
Space Center on the east coast of Florida.*

By finding and following her interests in math and science, and then in
the specialized area of optics, and sticking to her goals through hard work
and dedication, Ochoa had advanced to a high level in her field. Now she
would be able to apply her skills as a research scientist in a new job. After

graduating from Stanford, she applied for and was accepted to work at Sandia National Laboratories in Livermore, California, not too far from Stanford. She began working at this lab in 1985. Here she continued researching new and different optical systems that could be used for space travel. And when one of her brothers learned to pilot airplanes, she was inspired to join him. In 1986, she got a pilot's license to fly small-engine airplanes.

She was still interested in being an astronaut, and in 1987, she applied again. This time, she got close. Though she was not accepted to train to be an astronaut, she was in the top 100 out of the thousands of people who had applied. Often it takes many attempts to succeed at a goal, however, and Ochoa did not give up. She continued working at Sandia National Laboratories, playing the flute and volleyball in her spare time.

Her research work was successful but she still wanted to be an astronaut. In 1988, she got a little closer to her dream. She left her job at Sandia and took a position at NASA Ames Research Center at Moffett Federal Airfield in California. Though not training as an astronaut, she was now an employee of NASA. And her research would be used directly for the space shuttle program that she hoped to join one day.

After only a few months at Ames, she was **promoted**. An employee is promoted to a higher position for demonstrating success in his or her current job. In Ochoa's new position, she was leader of a team of 35 engineers and scientists.

Her ability to work with others was useful in her position as chief of the Intelligent Systems Technology Branch at Ames. Her team mainly

Sally Ride (right) and Kathryn Sullivan (left) demonstrate
a sleep restraint used by astronauts in space.

studied how to use robots in space. Sally Ride's team had used the robotic arm for the first time, and now Ochoa's team of researchers was working to perfect the use of this tool.

Ochoa balanced her busy work schedule with fun by playing the flute, riding her bicycle, and flying small planes. During this time, she met Coe

Fulmer Miles, a fellow research assistant at NASA. In 1990, they were married.

That same year, she received word of her acceptance into NASA's astronaut training program. More than 2,000 people had applied, and she was one of the 23 selected. This was a big achievement! Now her dream of going into space was much closer to coming true.

To travel into space, an astronaut must be skilled in many areas. Besides knowing about science and technology, the astronaut needs to be able to stay calm under pressure, have the ingenuity to solve any problems that come up, and most of all, have courage to go where few humans have gone before— space. Before she would have the opportunity to become the first woman of Mexican American heritage to go into space, Ochoa had to undergo a year of training.

Newly married, she and her husband left their home in California so she could attend training at the Johnson Space Center in Houston, Texas. This rigorous training program tests participants' skills and abilities to assure they will be successful astronauts. Ochoa had advanced degrees in science and engineering, but now she learned even more

Ellen Ochoa trained at the Johnson Space Center in Houston, Texas.

about other branches of science that could be useful for space travel, such as geology and astronomy. She also learned skills for surviving on both land and in water. The space shuttle program has made amazing advances, but astronauts still have to be prepared for any situation they might encounter on their missions into space.

Life & Career Skills

Ochoa had spent years preparing for her first trip into space. But in addition to the special training she received at NASA, her experience collaborating with others was valuable in space. A space shuttle crew lives and works together in close quarters for many days in a unique gravity-free environment. Knowing how to cooperate, share, and work together can make a big difference in the success of a mission. Growing up with three brothers and a sister probably taught Ochoa a lot about getting along with others! And playing the flute with a big orchestra was yet another way to practice working, and playing, with others.

She passed each area of the training program, and in July 1991, she became an astronaut. She was one of 110 people in the country at that time eligible to be selected for space missions. While waiting her turn, she used her background in engineering and optics to do research and development for the space exploration program at NASA. This was an exciting time. She was given two awards for her research, some of the many honors she would receive throughout her successful career with NASA.

Only two years after passing her training program, Ochoa was thrilled to be selected to join a team of astronauts for what would become her first mission into space. Then on April 8, 1993, Ellen Ochoa became the first Latina woman to travel into space. She was a mission specialist on a nine-day trip aboard the space shuttle *Discovery* and the only woman on the five-member crew.

Ellen Ochoa (far right) was the only woman on her first mission. Other crew members were (standing, from left) Kenneth D. Cockrell, Steven S. Oswald, (seated) C. Michael Foale, and Kenneth D. Cameron.

Their mission was to research the sun and its effects on Earth's environment using the ATLAS-2, which stands for Atmospheric Laboratory for Applications and Science-2, scientific payload. The payload is the cargo a vehicle carries. Her job was similar to Sally Ride's first job in space. Ochoa operated the robotic arm—or as NASA calls it, the remote

Ellen Ochoa's first space shuttle mission was a great success.

manipulator arm—to launch and retrieve a Spartan 201 satellite. The satellite weighed about 2,800 pounds (1,270 kilograms), and it orbited space on its own for two days before she brought it back to the shuttle.

She was excited to have accomplished her goal, and being in space was thrilling. She could look out the window of the space shuttle and see Earth! She had studied light and ways of seeing for many years, and now she noticed that Earth's colors were much brighter than even the photographs she had seen that were taken from space. The view out the window changed frequently because *Discovery*, like all space shuttles, traveled very fast, at about 5 miles (8 kilometers) per second, or about 18,000 miles (28,968 km) per hour.

Being weightless was also exciting. She said that because of the lack of gravity, your arms and legs look longer and thinner—you are even a little bit taller. On Earth, the pressure of gravity keeps everything on the ground. But in space, there is no gravity. Astronauts, along with everything onboard the space shuttle that isn't strapped down, float around inside the cabin. Because of this, day-to-day life is different in space. For example, on

21st Century Content

The space shuttle *Columbia* launched on April 12, 1981, and landed on April 14, 1981. This was the first flight of a space shuttle. The flight was called STS-1. NASA uses the STS system to number each mission into space. The letters stand for Space Transportation System. Ochoa's first mission into space was STS-56.

All of NASA's work, including space missions, is funded by the U.S. government. The government gets its money from taxpayers. So, when you are older and have a job, money to pay for taxes will be taken out of your paycheck. Some of that money may eventually be used to pay for NASA projects. Maybe by the time you are old enough to have a full-time job, your taxes will help pay for a human settlement on the moon—or on Mars!

The space shuttle Discovery *lands on April 17, 1993,
with Ochoa and other crew members aboard.*

Discovery, Ochoa slept inside a tiny compartment so that she would not float around while she was sleeping. And astronauts eat special food that can be prepared simply by adding water or heating in a small oven.

The *Discovery* orbited Earth 148 times before safely landing on April 17, 1993. Shortly after her return, Ochoa turned 35 years old. An accomplished scientist, engineer, and astronaut, she continued to work for NASA, developing software and optical systems that could be used in space exploration.

In 1994, she prepared for a second space mission. This time, her job was payload commander aboard the shuttle *Atlantis* on mission STS-66. One payload was a satellite called the CRISTA-SPAS. She once again used the robotic arm to launch and retrieve the satellite.

This time, the satellite orbited for eight days, collecting information about the sun and how its energy affects Earth's climate. The crew researched the depletion of the ozone layer, an area of Earth's atmosphere that protects the planet from the sun's ultraviolet rays. This space mission lasted from November 4 to November 14, 1994, and did not encounter any problems.

The next few years were busy ones for Ochoa. Her work became more widely recognized, and she received several awards and honors. She became a mother for the first time when she gave birth to her

Ochoa has always set high standards for herself and others have taken notice. She has received many honors and awards for her work. She was given Space Flight Medals from NASA for each of her first two missions into space. In 1993, she was honored with the Congressional Hispanic Caucus Institute's Medallion of Excellence. The next year, she received an Engineering Achievement Award and the Women in Aerospace Outstanding Achievement Award from Women in Aerospace, a nonprofit organization. She received NASA's Outstanding Leadership Medal in 1995 and the Exceptional Service Medal in 1997.

son, Wilson. She and her husband relished their first year with him. When Wilson was a year old, his mother was preparing for her third trip into space.

For her third flight, she was a member of the crew of STS-96 *Discovery*, the first mission to dock a spacecraft to the International Space Station (ISS), in 1999. ISS is a satellite in space where astronauts live and do research. It is like a scientific laboratory in space. It was part of Ochoa's mission to deliver supplies such as blankets, clothing, and medicine to ISS so that astronauts could stay there comfortably for longer periods of time.

Her most recent flight into space was STS-110 aboard the shuttle *Atlantis* in 2002 that docked to the ISS. She was once again responsible for controlling the robotic arm. For this mission, she unloaded materials that would be used to enlarge the ISS, such as trusses, which are arrangements of beams that form a rigid framework. She was in space for about 11 days.

On the ground, Ochoa works in robotics and space station development. She also serves as director of flight crew operations at the Johnson Space Center, where she directs the Astronaut Office and Aircraft Operations.

Ochoa continues to balance work and family life, similar to the way she balanced music and math as a child. She plays the flute and is active in sports such as volleyball and bicycling. Her family is very important to her, and she spends as much time as she can with her husband and two sons.

CHAPTER FOUR

A SHINING EXAMPLE

Ellen Ochoa (far left) and fellow astronauts Joan Higgenbotham (second from left) and Yvonne Cagle (third from left) give a presentation about women in space in 1999. Former astronaut Sally Ride stands at right.

Since she took her first trip into space, Ochoa has been invited to speak to students at hundreds of schools about her experiences as a scientist and astronaut. Though public speaking and being a role model to thousands of children are not things she considered when choosing to be an astronaut, she enjoys the experience and is generous with her time. She gave about 150 talks in her first few years as an astronaut.

Ellen Ochoa works hard to balance the demands of her home life and work life.

A strong believer in education, Ochoa is committed to the message her own mother taught her as a child. She tells children and teens to study hard and encourages each one to follow his or her dreams. She enthusiastically shares her message of perseverance and hard work with students. She talks to them about finding what they love to do and explains the nitty-gritty of life as an astronaut. For kids interested in science or math, she advises them to find out what jobs are available and what it takes to do the job they want to do. This way, kids can be prepared.

She says, "Stay in school. Education increases career options and gives you a chance for a wide variety of jobs. If you want to be an astronaut, get a college degree in a technical field such as science, math, or medicine. Either work for NASA or join one of the military services to learn more and work more in your chosen specialty."

One of the most important ways that Ochoa gives back to the community is by being a positive role model. She is a shining example of how one woman is able to be successful as a mother and a professional, even in a field in which women are rare. Ochoa is a trailblazer who has helped open

Ellen Ochoa's ability to work independently and her desire to go beyond the basics and continually master new skills have helped her achieve success in her career. Her example inspired the people of two communities to name schools in her honor. Ellen Ochoa Middle School opened its doors in Pasco, Washington, in 2002. The school even named its team the Rockets in honor of the exciting career of their school's namesake. Ellen Ochoa Learning Center is located in Cudahy, California, and serves children in prekindergarten through eighth grades. When Ochoa visited, the students treated her to a music and dance performance after she spoke to them about the importance of education and working hard in school.

Though it was a number of years ago that Ochoa was discouraged from studying electrical engineering, there is still a big difference in the numbers of men and women who enter careers in science and math. While girls often get good grades in math and science, statistics show they are less likely than boys to choose to take advanced courses in math and science that could expand their career choices.

Why to you think girls are less likely to take advanced courses in math and science? What do you think could be done to encourage more girls to take advanced math and science classes?

Ellen Ochoa and fellow mission specialist Rex Walheim on the space shuttle Atlantis.

doors for many. Watching her, young women and girls, especially from Latino backgrounds, can see that it's possible to realize their own dreams.

Of course, not everyone wants to become an astronaut or hopes for a career in math or science. But Ochoa tells girls that they can succeed in whatever they hope to do if they work hard. While there were not very many women in her engineering classes at Stanford, she says there are lots of women working at NASA.

When Ochoa became an astronaut, she probably wasn't thinking that the 1993 STS-56 mission would make her the first Latina in space—but it did. Some books call her the first Hispanic American woman astronaut in space; others say she is the first Latina. Both of these refer to the fact that Ochoa's grandparents immigrated to the United States from Mexico. Now, Ochoa says students don't seem to notice her cultural heritage or gender when she meets them. They just see an astronaut.

Ochoa wears many hats in her job at NASA. In addition to being an astronaut, designing computer systems, and conducting research on robotics and optical systems, she has represented NASA at conferences about space technology in Russia and other countries. A conference is a meeting where people get together to talk about one topic. Many countries, such as Russia and the United States, work together in the exploration of outer space.

Learning & Innovation Skills

The first Latino man in space, Franklin Chang-Diaz, was born in Costa Rica and educated in Costa Rica and the United States. Since becoming an astronaut in 1981, Chang-Diaz has been on seven missions in space and received numerous medals and awards. He has also designed and is constructing a rocket engine based on an innovative technology that could take a manned spacecraft to Mars in less than three months. That is amazing because with current technology, it would take more than nine months to reach Mars with a manned spacecraft.

CHAPTER FIVE

ENJOYING THE RIDE

The first image of the surface of Mars was taken by Viking 1
shortly after landing on the planet on July 20, 1976.

Ellen Ochoa has logged 978 hours in space! She has received numerous awards and medals for her outstanding achievements in aerospace. What will she do next?

Ochoa says she would like to fly to Mars or another planet. She also thinks it would be exciting to live on the International Space Station and research ways to live there using fuels available in space.

But it is also important to her that other astronauts have the opportunity to go into space. She decided against participating in more space missions, at least for now, so that other astronauts can have the chance to make the trip as she did. Being able to step aside and let others have that opportunity is as important to being a good leader as knowing when to take charge. Another part of Ochoa's job on the ground as director of Flight Crew Operations is deciding which astronauts are ready to make the trip into space.

Ochoa's example shows what traits make a successful astronaut. She is an experienced research engineer and pilot. She is able to cooperate

21st Century Content

Michael Lopez-Alegria, the first Latino to walk in space, was born in Spain and moved to the United States as a teenager. After his first trip in space, Lopez-Alegria served as NASA director of operations at the Yuri Gagarin Cosmonaut Training Center in Star City, Russia. In 2006–07, he also served as the commander of the International Space Station, living for six months in space.

Teams of astronauts live aboard the International Space Station for months at a time.

*Astronaut Sunita Williams on a spacewalk outside the
International Space Station on December 16, 2006.*

and to share with her crew. Her good grades and many scholarly
accomplishments demonstrate her ability to focus and concentrate, which
help her perform her many jobs, such as operating the robotic arm to

This view of the shuttle Discovery *was taken from Russia's Mir Space Station.*

Ochoa brought her flute with her on her first space mission. She played some of her favorite classical music, such as compositions by Mozart and Vivaldi. She even played the U.S. Marine Corps Hymn for Ken Cameron, a Marine Corps colonel who was commander of the space mission. Ochoa says that playing music in space "was just very peaceful." She also explains, "You can hold the music up and you don't even need a music stand."

If you went on a space shuttle mission, what is the one personal belonging that you would bring? Why?

retrieve a satellite. Her creativity allows her to look at problems from different angles and imagine many different solutions to challenging situations and research questions. It also comes in handy helping an astronaut get by for days in the small, gravity-free environment of the space shuttle.

Another important quality for an astronaut, as well as for following one's dreams for the future, is courage. Ochoa had to be very courageous to continue her education, apply to be an astronaut, go through the yearlong training, and then get into the shuttle and fly into space!

Courage, like these other qualities, is something that can be developed over time. And it is not just being an astronaut that takes courage. Trying anything new often takes courage.

Ochoa says that she is lucky; she loves her job and her family. Maybe it would be hard not to be happy with so many accomplishments, but there are people who have a hard time recognizing the positive in life. She appreciates the fun job that she has. Her journey—all the way around Earth—shows us how to follow our dreams, no matter what they might be, and to remember to enjoy the ride.

*Ochoa (seated center), pictured here with fellow STS-96 crew members
in 1999, currently serves as NASA's Director of Flight Operations.*

Timeline

1958   Ellen Ochoa is born in Los Angeles, California.

1969   Neil Armstrong becomes the first man to walk on the moon.

1975   Ellen is valedictorian at Grossmont High School.

1980   Ochoa receives her bachelor's degree from San Diego State University.

1981   NASA launches *Columbia*, the first space shuttle to travel into space and return to Earth. Ochoa receives her master's degree from Stanford University.

1983   Sally Ride becomes the first woman to travel into space.

1985   Ochoa receives her doctorate from Stanford University and begins her first job at Sandia National Laboratories as a research engineer.

1986   Ochoa trains for and receives her pilot's license to fly small airplanes.

1988   Ochoa begins working at NASA Ames Research Center at Moffett Federal Airfield, California.

1989   Ochoa receives the Hispanic Engineer National Achievement Award.

1990   Ochoa is accepted into the Astronaut Training Program at NASA. She marries Coe Fulmer Miles, a fellow research assistant at Ames (currently a patent attorney).

1992   Ochoa receives two Space Act Tech Brief Awards from NASA.

1993 Ochoa becomes the first Latina to travel in space as a crew member on the shuttle *Discovery*. She receives the Congressional Hispanic Caucus Institute's Medallion of Excellence.

1994 Ochoa takes her second trip into space as payload commander aboard the shuttle *Atlantis*. She receives two Space Flight Medals from NASA.

1995 Ochoa receives an Outstanding Leadership Medal from NASA.

1997 Ochoa receives an Exceptional Service Medal from NASA.

1999 Ochoa participates in NASA's first docking to the International Space Station on the shuttle *Discovery*.

2002 Ochoa makes her fourth mission into space aboard the shuttle *Atlantis*.

2006 Ochoa attends the naming ceremony for the Ellen Ochoa Learning Center in Cudahy, California.

Glossary

astronomy (uh-STRON-uh-mee) the scientific study of the universe and the motion, size, position, and relationship of objects in it

bilingual (bye-LING-gwuhl) fluent, or able to read and write, in two languages

cargo (KAR-goh) goods or a load of something carried by a vehicle

depletion (di-PLEE-shuhn) the emptying or loss of quantity of something

discrimination (diss-KRIM-uh-NAY-shuhn) unjust behavior to others based on differences such as race, age, or gender

diverse (duh-VURSS) varied, having many different kinds

doctorate (DOK-tuh-ret) the highest degree awarded by a college or university

engineering (en-juh-NIHR-eeng) the application of scientific knowledge to solve practical problems

geology (jee-OL-uh-jee) the scientific study of the earth, or another planet, but specifically the rocks, minerals, soil, and physical structure

inquisitive (in-KWIZ-uh-tiv) eager or excited to gain knowledge

Latina (lah-TEE-nuh) a woman of Latin American descent

optics (OP-tiks) the branch of scientific study that deals with sight and light

perseverance (pur-suh-VEER-ens) endurance, being able to stick with something for a long time

promoted (pruh-MO-ted) to be raised to a more senior level or position

satellites (SAT-uh-lites) objects that orbit a planet

validated (VAL-i-day-ted) to confirm something, or to show that something was true or worthwhile

FOR MORE INFORMATION

Books

Camp, Carole Ann. *American Women Inventors*. Berkeley Heights, NJ: Enslow Publishers, 2004.

Iverson, Teresa. *Hispanic American Biographies: Ellen Ochoa*. Chicago: Raintree Steck-Vaughn, 2006.

Romero, Maritza. *Ellen Ochoa: The First Hispanic Woman Astronaut*. New York: PowerKids Press, 1997.

Woodmansee, Laura S. *Women Astronauts*. Burlington, ON, Canada: Apogee Books, 2002.

Web Sites

Lemelson-MIT Program, Inventor of the Week
web.mit.edu/invent/iow/ochoa.html
Offers a biography focusing on Ochoa's education and inventions

NASA Kids Main Page
www.nasa.gov/audience/forkids/home/index.html
Includes information about astronauts, missions, and the solar system, as well as games and activities

Stanford University, School of Engineering
soe.stanford.edu/AR97-98/ochoa.html
Features a brief biography of Ochoa

INDEX

ABOUT THE AUTHOR

Annie Buckley is a writer, artist, and teacher. She has written books for kids about many topics such as yoga, creative writing, and heroic girls. She also writes about art and culture for magazines. Like Ochoa, Annie studied many subjects such as art, writing, psychology, and education, but she did not study math or science in depth. She enjoyed learning more about physics, engineering, and, most of all, space travel while researching Ochoa's fascinating life. Annie hopes this book will inspire all kids to follow their dreams.